BIRDWA
ON MULL

Written by
Pictured by Philip Snow

Brown & Whittaker
2011

Dedication

To Caroline, Bethan and Olivia for sharing our wonderful life on Mull and remembering Eric and Mike—for all the laughter in the early days with the eagles with the sunlit eye.

Foreword

Dr Mike Madders, still known widely here as the first "Birdman of Mull" originally wrote a version of this little book in the 1980s (*Birds of Mull*, Saker Press, 1987) along with Philip Snow who provided the illustrations and annotated maps. As popular as it was, it has sadly long since been out of print. Just before Mike's untimely death in 2009, we suggested to him that we revise and update it with new text and look. He readily agreed and this is the result. We hope he would have approved.

Acknowledgements

We wish to thank all those who play their part in protecting Mull & Iona's special wildlife; in particular, farmers and land-owners, NFUS, CalMac, FCS, SNH, Mull & Iona Community Trust, Strathclyde Police, Mull Bird Club, wildlife tour and boat operators and the RSPB. Mull Eagle Watch volunteers, visitors and the wider community do so much each year to protect the eagles. Finlay Christine, Iain Erskine, Sheila and Charlie Weir, Roger Broad and Debby Thorne have provided much needed support and friendship over the years. Thank you to all.

© *Text:* David Sexton
© *Illustrations:* Philip Snow

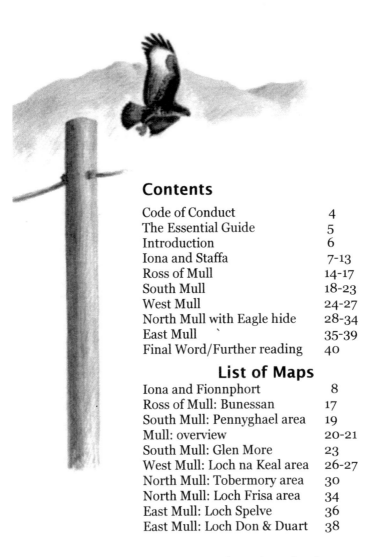

Contents

List of Maps

Cover picture: *White-tailed eagles talon grappling display, part of pair-bonding and common to the world's fish eagles*

ISBN 9781904353140

Published by Brown & Whittaker Publishing
Tobermory PA75 6PR
www.brown-whittaker.co.uk
Set in Georgia and printed in Tobermory, Scotland

Code of Conduct

This may all seem like common sense to many and it is part of the recognised Country Code (see *Outdoors on Mull & Iona* leaflet) but if you are new to this sort of countryside here are a few quick reminders. Please leave gates exactly as you find them. Avoid climbing over fences and walls or walking through grass crops - walk round the edge of a field if you have to. Keep away from all livestock. Keep dogs, even those on leads, far away from cattle, especially cattle with calves. If sheep are being gathered, stay in your car until they pass. Leave lambs alone even if they look lost or abandoned. The ewe will probably not be far away. If you really think there is a problem, report it at the nearest farm and let them deal with it.

We also want to make sure that the wildlife you are here to see goes about its daily life without disturbance or harassment. We will offer up some tried and tested suggestions to ensure that this is the case. Many of the species featured and the places they live and breed are also protected by Scottish and UK law. Please don't park in passing places or harass wildlife just to get a photograph. If you see a wildlife crime being committed call the police 01631 510501.

Finally, the tremendous variety of wildlife and habitats which we are lucky enough to have on Mull and Iona is here thanks to generations of care by farmers and land managers. Livestock farming helps support a wealth of wildlife. and we pay tribute in this book to the men and women who, come rain or shine, help make the islands what they are today.

The Essential Guide

Time of year

Whilst most people still visit between May and August, Mull and Iona is a year-round wildlife watching place. It can get busy in summer although the crowds coming off the ferry soon seem to disperse into the landscape. Autumn, winter and early spring can be fabulous times to visit, all bringing with them their own seasonal specialities, climate and atmosphere. As far as I am concerned, there is no off-season, Mull's main wildlife attractions are resident all year round and there are many good wildlife and boat operators to choose from.

Weather

Any weather at any time. Take your chances and check local forecasts. All I would say is that even if it looks rough out there and you think there is no point in going out, wrap up well and go anyway. The chances are it will change soon and one end of the island can be in sun when the other is under cloud. So don't let the weather put you off. If you are going out to sea, remember that it is nearly always colder on the water than on land.

Kit

Apart from suitable clothes, a good pair of binoculars is a must, a telescope on a tripod is almost a must and a good field guide should go with you at all times.

Getting around

Most roads on Mull and Iona are single track. A bit like wildlife watching there is a Code of Conduct when it comes to using these roads. Never block passing places or farm access gates even if you have just seen an otter or an eagle. Let the vehicle behind you pass as soon as possible and allow time for journeys on slow roads—kill your speed, not a sheep or an otter, and be aware of island life trying to go about its business.

Public transport

It is just about possible to "do" parts of Mull by public transport, but you will need to do a bit of planning ahead. Bowman's buses meet most of the ferries at Craignure in the summer and head north via Fishnish and Salen to Tobermory and south to Fionnphort (for Iona). They only meet selected boats in the winter, so check the timetable or call the CalMac or VIC office. There is also a bus from Tobermory to Calgary via Dervaig. There are a number of local taxis which might help you fill in the gaps, otherwise it is foot or pedal power.

Introduction

Welcome to the UK's premier wildlife watching location. Whether you are local born and bred, a more recent resident of Mull, Iona and their offshore islands or a visitor here, you will probably already know just how important this area is for some key species of UK wildlife. If you are a visitor, you may be here for the first time or maybe you are a regular commuter to these shores? Whatever the case, we hope your first visit to this wonderful place will not be your last. The birds, the animals, the landscape, the people and the local food and drink will keep drawing you back time and time again. This book is designed to help you get the most from your holiday and to help you maximise your chances of seeing (or at least hearing) Mull and Iona's best birds even if you are only here for a day or two, and the maps will guide you to the top spots. Time to get out there.

Iona and Staffa

Many are touched by the spirituality of Iona, many love the unhurried pace and the lack of cars. A summer's day on Iona, if you get the right weather, is quite simply a little taste of heaven. The white sand and shell beaches, the calm turquoise seas, the call of waders and seabirds and the occasional daytime rasp of a corncrake is what makes Iona special to me. After travelling through Mull under the shadow of its hills, stepping onto Iona is like stepping onto the machair of the Uists or Barra. It is like a little bit of the Outer Hebrides right on our doorstep and is best enjoyed after the last ferry pulls out from Iona heading back to Fionnphort, laden with day visitors. Then Iona comes into its own. A settled calmness seems to descend and you are left free to walk or cycle the lanes and tracks of this magical island.

In spring and summer, the calls of the resident rooks and jackdaws are everywhere (always keep an eye out for a wandering chough from Colonsay to the south - you just never know). On the shoreline, oystercatchers pipe and ringed plovers peep, while offshore, common and Arctic terns hover and plunge. Common gulls mob circling buzzards over the Sound of Iona while shags, kittiwakes and other gulls race back and forth through the Sound from Staffa to the open ocean beyond. Iona seems to pick up occasional rarities, so watch out. I've known bee-eater and hobby to pass through.

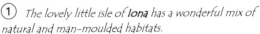

① *The lovely little isle of **Iona** has a wonderful mix of natural and man-moulded habitats.*

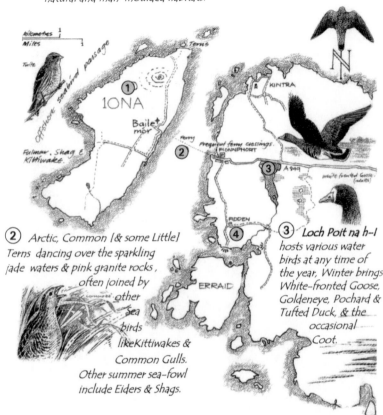

② *Arctic, Common [& some Little] Terns dancing over the sparkling jade waters & pink granite rocks, often joined by other sea birds like Kittiwakes & Common Gulls. Other summer sea-fowl include Eiders & Shags.*

③ **Loch Poit na h-I** *hosts various water birds at any time of the year, Winter brings White-fronted Goose, Goldeneye, Pochard & Tufted Duck, & the occasional Coot.*

④ **Fidden** *consists of a small area of flat farmland blending into typical lowland peat moor, opposite Iona & tidal Erraid, & particularly good for various wader & passerine.. Typical summer birds include Corncrake, Lapwing, Skylark & Sedge Warbler, & the occasional visiting Chough. Winter visitors from the far north include Barnacle Geese. Passage migrants can include other waders like Sanderling, Ruff, various stints, sandpipers & godwits, & they in turn attract raptors like Hen Harrier, Peregrine & Merlin.*

*On **Iona** itself, summer birds include the famous Corncrake. And at any time of year: Fulmar ,Petrels, Cormorant, Shelducks [except autumn], Common Buzzard, Ringed Plover, Lapwing, Herring & Black-backed Gulls, Jackdaw, Hooded Crow, Starling, Rock Dove, Linnet, Yellowhammer & Twite.. These can be joined temporarily on passage by such waders as Sanderling, Grey Plover, Black & Bar-tailed Godwits, & the odd Sandwich Tern.*

Iona's top bird is the corncrake, globally endangered and once heading to extinction here in Britain as a visiting breeding bird. It has been saved by pioneering research leading to sympathetic management action by farmers on the ground. Thanks to strenuous conservation efforts, corncrakes are once again on the increase. In some summers, 40 or so calling male birds make their presence felt during the key calling periods of May to July. Although they will sometimes give short daytime bursts of their craking, rasping "song" it is after dark (between midnight and 3 a.m. to be precise!) that they really let rip. That is when I am out doing my RSPB corncrake surveys, weaving my bike through the narrow lanes and farmyards of Iona, counting the calling males as I go and doing my best to avoid snarling sheepdogs and late night revellers from an island ceilidh.

FULMAR

GUILLEMOTS

RAZORBILL

BLACK GUILLEMOT
summer
& winter (below)

PUFFIN
summer
& winter

RAZORBILL
& GUILLEMOT
– winter

P Snow

Staffa

Staffa is owned and managed by the National Trust for Scotland and there are boat trips from Iona, Fionnphort and Ulva Ferry. Once arrived on Staffa, the spectacular geological formations of columnar basalt and the romance of Fingal's Cave absorb the eye and mind, but there is much to be seen on the outward and homeward passages. Skippers and crew will point out most birds of interest on the way. You will probably see common seals hauled out on rocky skerries and small islands just offshore from Mull as you gently ease your way up the Sound of Iona. It won't be long before you are seeing puffin, guillemot and razorbill on the water or streaming past the boat on a food flight. Kittiwakes, gulls and great skuas or bonxies are regularly seen (a pair or two of bonxies attempt to nest each year on Staffa) and you will see these bully boys (and girls) of the sea throttling auks or chasing them until they throw up their hard won catch. Not always something you want to witness during a rough sea crossing.

I have seen minke whale on the trip to Staffa and others have seen orca attacking porpoise just offshore so anything is possible. Rarities like white-billed diver have been reported from the route, but the more regularly seen great-northern diver are far more frequent in early spring. Look out for that give-away sign of a "hurry" of feeding gulls, terns, auks and gannets which might suggest something much bigger feeding below the surface.

Your boat will put you ashore for an hour or two. If it is puffins you are after, make sure you have got your timing right. They are only on land and nesting from May to July although you may occasionally see them on the sea at other times. But beware, one day they are there, the next they have gone, so always check with the skipper. Once landed, head straight for the area on the east side of the island which you will be directed to by the crew. The puffins may all be on the water just waiting for your visit! Why? Well, when you take up your position on the cliff top (well back from the over-hanging and crumbling edge), your presence will tend to keep puffin predators like bonxies and great black-backed gulls at bay. This allows the puffins to come in to their nest burrows unmolested. They will take off from the sea and wheel around in a big flock and eventually, after various false starts, one then two, then ten and then all of them will start landing close by, giving you the chance for some close-up photography or simply watching them close-to. They are stunning and interesting to watch but keep well back from any nest burrows and do not be tempted to creep ever closer or else you might send them all off again, much to the annoyance of your fellow puffin watchers or worse, into the beak of a passing bonxie.

Key species and where to watch

Corncrake : Head up from the Iona ferry ramp, turn left and follow the shore road. The fields to your right in June and July are growing silage. By the fire station is a good place to pause and watch and listen and gaze out across the colourful mix of flag iris, nettle, ragged robin and cow parsley. This is corncrake heaven (or "early cover" as it is known) and several birds will be hiding in its midst. It is where they will have come when they first migrated to Iona from Africa at the end of April. You have just got to be patient. Stand, watch and listen. Scan with eyes and binoculars. Never be tempted to climb the fence and walk through the field. Apart from crop and habitat damage, it is against the law to disturb a Schedule I species. The same applies to imitating their strange calls to try and entice them out. This is illegal and it disturbs the birds. So back to good old fashioned fieldcraft and patience . . . Occasionally one will hop up onto a wall or boulder, preen for a few minutes, maybe call once or twice and then disappear again into the jungle. If you put time in, you will be rewarded. Another good place to take a rest and watch the world go by (with a good chance of seeing a corncrake) is to turn right up past the ferry ramp either past the Argyll Hotel or Columba Hotel and head through the gate to the area between the Abbey and the sea. Find a comfortable grassy knoll, lean back against the stone dyke and wait. Watch the bare sheep trails through the iris beds as a corncrake may cross over and, again, keep an eye on any walls or boulders. The sheep should all have been removed from these areas by June to allow the vegetation and the corncrake habitat to flourish. It is this, cutting of the fields late in August or September (and from the inside of the field outwards so birds are eased out of the way and not chopped up in the middle) that constitutes the "Corncrake Friendly" mowing which farmers and crofters are paid for. This also benefits a host of other wildlife and plantlife. Late April and May can be a great time to see these elusive birds as they creep through the undergrowth. The organic garden of the Columba Hotel is a good tip: the corncrakes love it in there and who can blame them, but watch from the road. Good luck!

Twite: often in pairs in spring or family groups in summer or mixed finch flocks in autumn and winter. The lane across the centre of the island is a good place to watch for them.

Waders: the beaches, machair and wet flushes of Iona (and the area around Fidden on Mull on the opposite side of the Sound) make this the best area for breeding waders in the two islands. Redshank and snipe, lapwing and curlew in the damp pastures with ringed plovers on the beaches fill the air with their cries and occasional alarm calls if you are inadvertently too close to a nest. If you settle down on the beach for a picnic and a ringed plover is plaintively "peeping" its distress call at you while occasionally running to and fro, the chances are that you are sitting within a few metres of (if not right next to) a clutch of eggs on the sand and pebbles. They are so well camouflaged that they are easy to miss. Time to get up and move your picnic carefully and let the bird resume incubation.

Iona and Staffa top tips

Hire a bike and explore the island tracks and roads at your leisure.

Have a late night stroll on a summer's evening to hear corncrakes in full song and drumming snipe.

If you do not want to or cannot get off the boat at Staffa, do not despair. Often the skipper will take you on a personalised tour all around the island and you may see a basking shark. different caves and amazing geology. And you will still see puffins on the sea.

Gt Skua & A. Tern   P Snow ©

Ross of Mull

Although strictly speaking it is just the far tip of the long southern arm of Mull that is the Ross, for most people it is the whole of the long arm from Kinloch to Fionnphort that is The Ross. Listed below are some of my favourite spots, but there are many more which you can discover for yourself. The overall impression of the landscape is one of rugged and untamed beauty. Sure, man has been here and affecting the landscape for thousands of years, but somehow his impact on the land has been gentler and more sympathetic than elsewhere.

There are still working crofts and small holdings, there is only limited forestry and there is good native woodland and scrub cover. One such area is the community woodland at Tireragan where hazel, willow and birch abound, providing home to Irish hares, hen harrier, short-eared owl and good hunting for the Ross' pairs of golden eagles - a sign of what good ecological things can happen when grazing is kept well managed. It is the sort of welcome productive wildlife habitat that some fear when they talk of "scrub", a "jungle" or "wilderness" that might result if grazing animals are reduced. This is no wilderness but it is a haven and, at times, a blessed relief from the short cropped grasses, bracken forests and denuded heather of the open hill elsewhere on Mull. Of course, it is the whole mix of habitats, grazed and ungrazed, woodland and hill, mountain top and shoreline which gives the Ross of Mull (and the island generally) its distinctive character and makes it the wildlife-rich place it is.

Lapwings breeding - ♀ left & ♂ right. Fidden, Mull

Onwards up the Ross

Just outside Fionnphort, take the turn to Fidden. There is no better place on a summer's evening to listen for corncrake than the campsite at the farm. These are the first pioneers of a small population slowly getting re-established on Mull thanks to the efforts of the local farmer and the RSPB.

The farm here is one of the best on the island for looking after wading birds like lapwing and snipe as well as carrying out specific management for corncrakes. In winter, this area also hosts the island's important geese populations, including scarce Greenland white-fronted and barnacle as well as resident greylag, which are less welcome to the farmer. These flocks are always worth a scan in case other species of geese get caught up with them, like the occasional pink-foot, snow or brent. All in all, birdwatching from this road or taking a stroll along the beach will be one of the most re-warding ways to spend a few hours.

As you leave Fionnphort, the first body of water you will encounter is the freshwater Loch Pottie. Apart from the greylag geese, in winter there may be a few whooper swans, wigeon, pochard, tufted duck, teal and mallard and usually little grebes in the reeds. A coot would be an extreme rarity! You may be lucky and see an otter here too. The drive to Uisken beach ends in a beautiful sandy bay. In the summer, ringed plovers will be on the beach and this is always another possible area for corncrakes. Further on, Loch Assapol to the south of the main road is always worth a look. If the Greenland white-fronted geese are not at Fidden, they may be here. In the not too distant past, a pair of chough could be seen feeding in these fields and wheeling about above the cliff tops. Sadly, after ten years of trying unsuccessfully to rear chicks, they fizzled out as a breeding species, but we live in hope that one day they will re-colonise from nearby Colonsay which, on a clear day, looks just a few chough wing beats away. Look closely at any small flocks of feeding rooks or crows. You never know your luck! And listen for that typical loud and echoing "chhheeow" call not unlike an exaggerated jackdaw. Maybe you will be the first to record them again in this area? Let us know if you do!

The old road along the coast of Ardtun which you can join in Bunessan, is a good detour. This area still has working crofts and again, this less intensive style of farming means that many typical farmland finches and passerines still thrive. The breathtaking Wilderness looks incredibly close and, scanning the far skyline for an hour or two should yield soaring eagles - albeit at a distance. The Wilderness was the last place on Mull that white-tailed eagles nested in the 1870s before they became extinct, though even here they were not safe. Thank goodness they are now back on Mull and you are as likely to pick up a soaring sea eagle from this vantage point as you are a golden eagle. And just offshore there will be wandering auks from Staffa - guillemots, razorbills, even puffins as well as shags and gannets diving in the entrance to Loch Scridain.

At the eastern end of the Ross, is Pennyghael and the turn-off to Carsaig. This road is not for the faint-hearted and parking at the end can be seriously difficult. But if you do make it, the walk along the shoreline towards the Carsaig Arches is rough going but rewarding and you may well see golden eagle along the cliff tops, often being mobbed by buzzard, raven, kestrel and peregrine. Hen harriers quarter the rough ground on either side of the road.

At Pennyghael the coast of Loch Scridain is all excellent otter habitat. At low tide scan the mudflats in front of the Kinloch Hotel for greenshank, redshank, dunlin, lapwing and the occasional sea eagle. With the backdrop of Ben More, this is one of the best views on the island and well worth a long, lingering watch.

Key species and where to watch
Corncrakes, waders, gulls, Greenland white-fronted geese, barnacle geese: Fidden/Erraid/Knockvologan

Winter wildfowl species, otter Loch Pottie

Passerines, finches, corncrake, views to the Wilderness: Old Road/Ardtun/Bunessan

Farmland birds, skylark, waders: Uisken/Ardalanish

Geese, chough?: Loch Assapol/Scoor

Otters, eagles, hen harrier: Pennyghael/Carsaig

Ross of Mull Top Tips
Camp at Fidden Farm and let the summer calls of snipe, corncrake, and lapwing lull you off to sleep.

If you want a quiet road, avoid the main bus runs morning and afternoon as they are heading for Iona or back to Craignure.

① *In the attractive enclosed bay & village of **Bunessan**. One of the best viewpoints apart from the pub window!] is the parking area at the west end of the village, where typical sea-fowl, like all 3 divers, Eiders & Red-breasted Mergansers can be seen at various times of year.*

KEY:
꙰ viewpoints
deciduous wood / scrub.
coniferous forestry.
Ⓟ parking.

Lochna Lothaich

PENNYGHAEL→

A 849

BUNESSAN

LOCH ASSAPOL

UISKEN Ⓟ

② *Assapol House boasts one of Mull's rare Rookeries, & occasional rarer wildfowl like Long-tailed Duck & Scoters can end up on the loch, especially after gales. Winter wildfowl include: Whooper Swan, White-fronted & Greylag Geese, Goldeneye, Tufted Duck & Pochard.*

③ ***Uisken** is a great little bay with a magnificent view, especially south to the Paps of Jura.*

E Pochard & Tufted ducks.

Noisy Oyster Catchers, & peeping Ringed Plovers, are often found on the little beach, whilst offshore, Eiders & various divers can often be seen fishing [especially in winter]. In summer it can also boast the odd Corncrake rasping away in any iris beds. You may even see a corncrake.

Walk from Carsaig along the shore towards the Arches and back, or eastwards to Loch Buie. A stunning part of the coastline.

South Mull

At the T-junction just beyond the Kinloch Hotel you can turn left and follow the 'scenic route' to Salen to embark on one of the world's most beautiful drives. The road hugs the northern shore of the loch and you could spot an otter at any moment. If you do, try and avoid the temptation to jam the brakes on and leap out of the car or to start reversing, or you will blow this opportunity. If you are lucky enough to spot an otter, try to keep gently moving forward and wait for it to dive in its own time as it carries on fishing. Watch from a distance as it resurfaces, relaxed and undisturbed. If spooked they swim underwater for some distance, close to the shore and disappear into the bladderwrack at the water's edge. You don't need to get that close-up photograph; just watch and enjoy.

Soon the road turns away from the loch and up through Glen Seilisdeir, the 'glen of the irises.' As the road heads due north, you emerge from the dark corridor of conifers out onto open hill ground. Watch for cattle, sheep and deer on the road. As the road goes steeply down there is one of the best views, if not the best view on the island as a great archipelago of islands stretches out before you.....Inchkenneth, Ulva and Little Colonsay, with the Treshnish Islands and Staffa beyond...on a summer's or winter's evening this view will take your breath away.

Ptarmigans moulting into spring plumage, & Golden Plover.

The **Inner Reaches** are very shallow with rather a stony bed & only scattered areas of estuarine mud, silt & indented salt marsh,

where shaggy Highland cattle can obligingly pose by the old humpy road bridge. Shorebirds are a little limited, although Lapwing breed, & Dunlin & Ringed Plover can be temporarily plentiful whilst on spring or autumn passage.

① **Loch Scridain**

is a typical tidal loch of low, rocky & sea-weedy margins, a great place for specialities like divers & Eiders. . Gannets, can be found fishing quite close inshore in late spring & summer. One of the very best places to see all three regular Eurasian divers - but if you want to view them in their splendid breeding dress, the more uncommon two usually leave by late May.

③ **Carsaig Bay** only gradually reveals its spectacular setting as you slowly wind down the high road from Pennyghael, alongside tumbling waterfalls. Red Deer are regulars, joined on the summer high tops by plaintive Golden Plover.

There is some fine mixed woodland by the old pier, where tracks afford good views of cliff & coastal birds, like the declining, ['pure'] Rock Dove. The paths west, both low & high level, are particularly attractive, especially if eagles are 'wind-hanging' above the cliffs of Gorrie's Leap.

N

CALGARY DERVAIG

TORLOISK

TRESHNISH
ISLES

ULVA

STAFFA

Red
Deer

IONA ferry

FIONNPHORT

Loch
Assapol

UISKEN

©P.SNOW

TOBERMORY

CH
RISA

MORVERN

* Ards
River   LOCHALINE

SALEN   ferry
              Fishnish
              Bay

              Scallastle
              Bay

              CRAIGNURE

MULL   LOCHDON   ferry to
                            OBAN

* Ben More

PENNYGHAEL

CARSAIG   LOCHBUIE

Glen More

If you continue on the main road at the T-junction just beyond the Kinloch Hotel you will head straight on into the heart of Glen More. This place inspires different emotions in people. Some find it dark and forbidding, where the legend of the headless horseman can appear all too believable on dark winter nights. But for others, it is a glen of great grandeur, with impressive cliffs and crags. It is one of the best places on the island to sit, wait and watch for eagles. This whole area is 'Eagle Central.' A good place to stop is at the highest part of the glen where there is a marked parking area overlooking 'the three lochs.' There can be few days in good or even inclement weather when a scan of the ridges will not reveal a soaring or hunting golden or white-tailed eagle. There will also be hen harrier, kestrel, raven and possibly short-eared owl hunting below the parking area. Autumn is one of the best times to see eagle soaring activity when the adults are joined on the wing by still partially dependent juvenile birds with all birds soaring higher and more frequently in the winter when they are more reliant on carrion.

Key species and where to watch
Golden eagle, white-tailed eagle, curlew, short-eared owl, raven, and up in the hills, ptarmigan: Glen More/Ben More

White-tailed eagle, buzzard, golden eagle, hen harrier: Glen Seilisdeir

South Mull Top Tips
Have your flask of coffee at the parking area above the three lochs. On a good day you'll see it all from here: eagles, short-eared owls displaying in summer and snow buntings in winter.

In the narrows of Loch Beg as it joins Loch Scridain, you may also see common seal, the occasional grey seal, even minke whale. In recent years we've even seen a couple of rare northern bottle-nosed whales, so you just never know. Greenshank may be there at low tide along with redshank, red-breasted merganser, wigeon, shag and oystercatcher. This is also one of the best spots on the island to watch for hen harrier.

Find a high point overlooking Loch Scridain and scan for cetaceans like porpoise and minke whale, and look for seals and eagles on offshore skerries.

This superb area combines mountain, moorland, glen, forestry & freshwater loch, & consequently, a rich variety of birds. **Glen More** itself is about 16 km long & overlooked by many hills rising to over 2000 ft, with one of the best views of Ben More.

With several well-placed viewpoints, & sections of old road, it is one of the best places to see speciality upland birds. Typical birds in **spring & summer** include: Eagles, Hen Harrier, C. Buzzard, Merlin, Kestrel, Short-eared Owl, Cuckoo, Skylark, Wheatear, Whinchat & Stonechat,

Glen Forsa, cutting off to the north, can similarly produce good eagle sightings & the usual limited number of forestry species.

✱ Marks some of the best places to scan open spaces of hill & side glens, especially for Goldies. The scattered & more open areas of forestry are good for Hen Harriers, Short-eared Owls,& passerines like Whinchat & Stonechat. Late summer & autumn are the best times to see soaring Golden Eagles, especially with juveniles alongside practising their aerobatic skills, or all ranging widely for carrion, an important winter food source.

② **Loch Uisg**, to the south, is a sheltered freshwater loch with typical winter diving duck like Goldeneye & Pochard, & the charming Little Grebe or Dabchick, all year. LAGGAN

① The exposed, tidal **Loch Buie** has various typical species, especially fishing Red-throated Diver in summer, & many other divers & seafowl in winter. It also marks to start of the splendid walk to Carsaig, & several other shorter paths.

Ptarmigan, though not common here, can be seen on some of the hills that border Glen More. In winter, snow buntings occasionally feed on grit along the roadside.

West Mull

If I had to choose, west Mull is probably my favourite area of the island. The beauty and starkness of the landscape along Loch na Keal, the Gribun cliffs, Loch Ba and the view from Killiechronan is awe-inspiring in any season, in any weather, at any time of day. The drives north across from Glen Seilisdeir or from Salen west along Loch na Keal are equally dramatic although there is nothing that quite compares with being at sea level under the precipitous Gribun cliffs. Peregrines may call out from the cliff tops as you scan across the winter sea to Inch Kenneth or Eorsa in search of sea eagles. Great northern divers and Slavonian grebes will still be there in early spring having assumed their stunning breeding plumage before heading north.

On the south side of Loch na Keal, check out Scarisdale rocks for otters and sea eagles and, round at Killiechronan, pull in near to the campsite and watch for wintering wildfowl - goldeneye, wigeon, mergansers and goosanders and sea eagles lounging about on the beach. Iceland and glaucous gulls are regulars at the fish farm outflow at Knock and it is a great place to watch the eagles hunt.

Further west, from Ulva Ferry, you can get boat trips to the Treshnish Islands and Staffa, over to Ulva or into Loch na Keal. On the Treshnish Islands you can spend a few blissful hours ashore in the company of thousands of seabirds – puffins, guillemots (watch for "bridled" ones), razorbills, and shags along with gulls, wheatears, the occasional corncrake and basking sharks offshore. One summer, a boat trip watched in awe as a pod of orcas chased, caught and ate a porpoise alongside their boat. You never know what will turn up when you are out there. As with Staffa, please give the puffins some space.

The fields around Ulva ferry and towards Lagganulva are excellent for waders - lapwing, curlew and snipe. You may also see golden eagle over the hills.

G.n. Divers; adult spring & 1st winter birds.   *RSnow 87*

Key species and where to watch

Divers, grebes, sea eagles, eiders, red-breasted mergansers, goldeneye, winter gulls, otters: Loch na Keal

Golden eagle, grey heron, oystercatcher, kestrel, hen harrier, peregrine: Ulva

All the auks, fulmar, shag, great skua, corncrake, twite and cetaceans, basking shark, arctic skua: Treshnish Islands

West Mull top tips

On the south shore of Loch na Keal, look seaward for otters and towards Ben More for soaring eagles.

Watch for sea eagles going in for a spot of otter watching on the reefs at Scarisdale or from the campsite at Killiechronan.

Enjoy the tranquillity of Ulva, a place without traffic.

Red throated Divers at nest

Typical birds at **any time of year** include: Shag, Eider, Grey Heron, Red-breasted Merganser, Curlew, O. Catcher & Redshank.

① **Eas Fors** comprises three fine waterfalls tumbling down into the sea loch, home for most of the year to Dipper & Grey Wagtail.

② **Ulva** combines fine mixed woodland with the usual attractions of a small Hebridean isle, & can be reached by fairly regular ferries in the summer. This is the best time for vocal visitors like Wood Warbler & Tree Pipit, whilst Common & Arctic Terns often fish the narrow strait.

② & ③ Winter brings in those typical northern wildfowl, Barnacle Geese, to feed on low lying grassy peninsulas like Ulva Ferry.

④ Opposite I. Kenneth, & proceeding westwards, the towering volcanic cliffs of **Gribun** & **Balmeanach** lead ones eyes inevitably towards the magnificent cliffs & headland of the Wilderness. As ever, such heights are home to C. Buzzard, Kestrel & Raven.

From viewpoint ⑤ above Mackinnon's Cave, seabirds like Shag, Fulmar & Kittiwakes. In **winter** they are joined by such as: Gt. Northern & Black-throated Divers, Slavonian Grebe, Wigeon, Mallard, Goldeneye, Razorbill & Black Guillemot. Scotland's infamous 'telephone pole eagle', the Common Buzzard, often perches around here to fight over road kills [rabbits etc] with Hooded Crow & Raven.

(9) *Scarisdale Rocks* are usually a low tide haul out for Common Seals & off duty Shags - & Otters are often around, too. In recent years White-tailed eagles have been seen scavenging dead sheep or deer, washed down the river onto the shore. The oak & birch woods have Redstart & Tree Pipit which still nest, as they do on the north side at

Kellan Woods **(6)**, with other summer visitors like G. S. Woodpecker, Treecreeper, Wood Warbler & various tits.

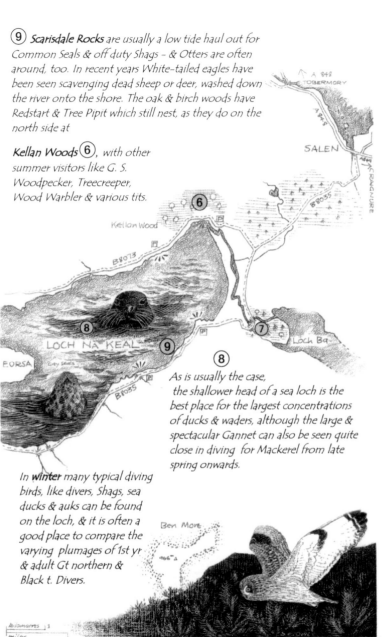

(8) As is usually the case, the shallower head of a sea loch is the best place for the largest concentrations of ducks & waders, although the large & spectacular Gannet can also be seen quite close in diving for Mackerel from late spring onwards.

In **winter** many typical diving birds, like divers, Shags, sea ducks & auks can be found on the loch, & it is often a good place to compare the varying plumages of 1st yr & adult Gt northern & Black t. Divers.

(7) The shady footpath through the estate to Loch Ba adds several more different birds like Goldcrest, Redpoll, & Coal Tit, & Dippers are usually on the river by the old road bridge. The summer shoreline of the large freshwater loch is fine for Common Sandpipers, & views, if distant, can be had of Red-throated Divers.

North Mull

North Mull is a place to meander and enjoy the wildlife and the scenic delights of Calgary, Loch Cuin at Dervaig, Loch Frisa (Scottish home of the white-tailed eagle), Mishnish Lochs, Glengorm and Aros Park on the outskirts of Tobermory.

Calgary Bay can be busy in summer and because the bay is so heavily used and the dunes and machair are fragile, it is important to respect the environment and follow the rules regarding litter and dogs. Early morning and late evening are quiet times to visit. Otters frequent the bay all the year round, basking sharks cruise back and forth in the summer and both species of eagle regularly break the skyline for those lying back on the white sand beach scanning the ridges. There are buzzards galore, red-throated divers feeding out in the bay along with a good selection of eider, red-breasted merganser, shags and guillemots. Every year, delicate, fluttering sand martins, those early-arriving, long-distance summer migrants arrive to try and nest in the sand banks in the dunes. They have just flown from Africa to herald the spring and summer in Mull and need peace to nest. Check before you picnic or run around the dunes that you are nowhere near the little holes in the sandbanks that betray where they are nesting.

Over the hills to Dervaig, either by the main road or by the hill road from Torloisk. The hill road passes through hen harrier, merlin, short-eared owl and red grouse country. There are still a few grouse to be seen here, although these often wet west coast islands have never been good for grouse.

Short eared Owl
& Hen Harrier.

PSnow©

Sitting at the high point on the road and looking out towards the distant Treshnish Islands offers a splendid panorama all round.

♂ & ♀ Hen Harriers, log nest site   P. Snow

On the main road, you will pass the turn off to Croig where I saw my first wild otter over 30 years ago - and they are still there! At Dervaig, a scan of Loch Cuin may pick up green-shank, redshank, dunlin and a range of familiar waterfowl. Continuing on the Tobermory road, you will pass the turn off for the Sea Eagle Hide (see pp 32-33) and the Mishnish Lochs where family groups of whooper swans are regular visitors in autumn, winter and early spring as they stop off *en route* to and from Iceland. Dabchicks bob about in the shallows, grey-lag geese families gather here to moult (watch out for the Loch Frisa eagle pair hunting here - greylag adult and gosling are favourite menu items) and there is a gull bathing and gathering spot at the north end.

Winding down into Tobermory, a turn to the left will take you to Glengorm and good raptor country with a walk to the coast at Ardmore where you can search for basking sharks off the point. On the southern outskirts of Tobermory, the walks in Aros Park go through impressive policy woodland, past dramatic waterfalls and around the loch, home to dippers, grey wagtail, goldeneye and even an occasional kingfisher in winter. The woodlands have great-spotted woodpecker, coal tit, tawny owl and all the expected summer migrants - wood warbler, tree pipit and redstarts. Tobermory itself has its own wildlife. You may see an otter in the bay and, where the river flows out into the bay, you may see dipper, grey wagtail, eider and an occasional winter "white-winged" gull (Iceland and glaucous).

Tobermory's colourful little harbour & ferry port is justly one of Mull's 'other' main attractions, also providing a good centre for various walks & habitats with yr round bird interest. ② The busy bay can be viewed from several viewpoints &

levels, & noted for winter, 'white-winged' Iceland & Glaucous Gulls. A fine little stream waterfalls down into the south side of the bay from Aros Park [beyond the pontoons], Grey Wagtails can often be seen stalking the beach.

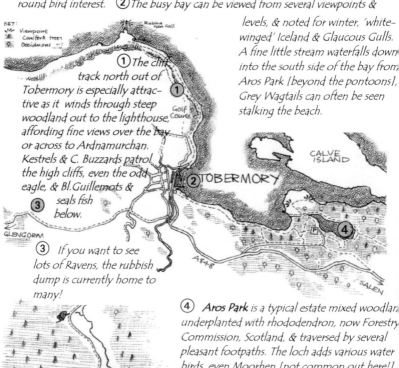

① The cliff track north out of Tobermory is especially attractive as it winds through steep woodland out to the lighthouse, affording fine views over the bay or across to Ardnamurchan. Kestrels & C. Buzzards patrol the high cliffs, even the odd eagle, & Bl. Guillemots & ③ seals fish below.

③ If you want to see lots of Ravens, the rubbish dump is currently home to many!

④ **Aros Park** is a typical estate mixed woodland underplanted with rhododendron, now Forestry Commission, Scotland, & traversed by several pleasant footpaths. The loch adds various water birds, even Moorhen [not common out here!] the many woodland birds. They include: Pheasant, Woodcock, Tawny Owl, G-s. Woodpecker, thrushes, tits, Treecreeper, Siskin, Redpoll & Bullfinch.

⑤ The three **Mishnish Lochs** are well stocked with Brown Trout, & thus also very attractive to avian fishers! Red-throated Divers, Little Grebe, Grey Heron, Mallard R-b. Mergansers – even the rarer Goosander – can be seen most anytime of the yr, joined in winter by Goldeneye, & 'grazing' Whooper Swans. Lochside vegetation & scrub further attracts passerines like Reed Bunting, whilst on the sparsely forested slopes above, H. Harriers & other raptors can be seen.

Key species and where to watch

Golden eagle: Calgary Bay north ridge, Torloisk hill road, north end of Loch Frisa

White-tailed eagle: Loch Frisa

Dipper: Aros Bridge, Aros Park, Loch Cuin, Tobermory river (near Tobermory Distillery)

Short-eared owl, hen harrier, merlin: Torloisk hill road, Glengorm

Greenshank, redshank, other waders: Loch Cuin

Otter: Calgary Bay, Loch Cuin, Croig, Tobermory Bay

North Mull top tips

A special ranger-led trip to the famous Eagle Hide at Loch Frisa.

A sunset barbeque at Calgary listening for late night corncrakes from the fields at the back of the bay.

A quiet evening stroll at Croig watching for otters and listening to snipe 'drumming' at dusk.

Watch for barn owls quartering the rough ground around Loch Cuin.

Watch 'sky-dancing' hen harriers from the Torloisk hill road.

Rubha nan gall. Peregrine.

The Eagle Hide

No trip to Mull is complete without a trip to Loch Frisa, owned and managed by the Forestry Commission Scotland - and to the world-renowned Eagle Hide. As far as we know this brilliant facility is the only permanent hide anywhere on the planet which overlooks the nesting area of a pair of wild white-tailed eagles. The area and the eagles - when they are nesting successfully - can act as a 'honey pot' and help take the pressure off other pairs of sea eagles which are generally left alone to get on quietly with nesting away from public view. There may be other projects which start up in the future but the Loch Frisa hide will always be the original and best.

The regular pair of eagles which nest here is a female called Frisa (hatched in Mull in 1992) and her lifetime mate Skye (where he was hatched in 1994). They first paired up in 1997 and have been nesting regularly at Loch Frisa since 1998. They have successfully raised many chicks, some of which are now breeding elsewhere in Scotland and have been the subjects of many television programmes over the years, especially BBC's Springwatch and Autumnwatch.

A unique viewing and protection partnership called 'Mull Eagle Watch' helps to ensure the eagles breed without disturbance. The partnership is made up of the Forestry Commission Scotland, RSPB Scotland, the Mull & Iona Community Trust, Scottish Natural Heritage and Strathclyde Police. The excellent viewing hide is mobile and can be positioned anywhere along the forestry track to give visitors the best chance of seeing the eagles assisted by binoculars, telescopes and often CCTV.

Access and meeting points can change from year to year, depending on where the eagles nest, so always check with the Visitor Information Centres or leaflets – beware old, out of date leaflets in B&Bs as you may end up at the wrong meeting point, missing the trip. Trips are often twice a day and in groups of up to 30. There is no vehicular access up the forestry track unless you're booked on a trip. Prices are very modest and all income goes back to the local Mull Community Trust for distribution to local good causes and to the Mull Eagle Watch project. The trips, led by experienced rangers last about two hours and you stand a very good chance of seeing the sea eagles all year round. Golden eagles, ravens, peregrine, buzzard, and hen harrier are all regularly seen too.

❶ *White-tailed eagle*
❷ *Golden eagle*
❸ *Common buzzard*

It's simply one of the best wildlife watching experiences you can have on Mull and is not to be missed. Check for local booking details and other wildlife trips with the Visitor Information Centre at Craignure.

DERVAIG

Adult White-tailed or Sea Eagles

TOBERMORY

B 8073

MISHNISH LOCHS

The **White-tailed Eagle** nest is liable to move from yr to yr, but the hide is usually somewhere near here.

(1) Note hide access is strictly only by official vehicles & prebooking, or footpath access for walkers or cyclists.

N

Red Deer in 'velvet'

A848 TOBERMORY

Speinne Beag

Hare (late winter coat)

LOCH FRISA

DERVAIG

SALEN FOREST

(2) **Salen Bay** is particularly famous for its Common Seal haul-out on the little skerries, & Otters – but please do not block the narrow road to view them [there are several little parking spaces]! There is also a fine view across to Morvern from many parts of this road north, & the chance of divers, & occasional Minke Whales, heading through the Sound.

GLEN AROS

AROS RIVER

(4)

AROS

(3)

SALEN BAY

(2)

SALEN

A848

OTTERS & COMMON SEALS

(3) There are several viewpoints for the charming little **Aros Estuary**, with its humpy old road bridge, waterside cottages & commanding castle ruins. Typical waterbirds include Grey Heron, Shelduck [except autumn], R-b. Mergansers, the usual waders, plus Wigeon etc in the winter.

(4) **Glen Aros** is a fine glen for sightings of both eagle sps, & many other birds, plus Red Deer, & the odd Irish Hare. The Aros River initially flows right by its little road into Aros Bay, & thus Dipper & other waterbirds can be enjoyed along its short length, & on the shore in winter.

East Mull

For many, it is the softer east coast of Mull which offers some of the best bird watching opportunities. The road around Loch Spelve towards Croggan and then south via the freshwater Loch Uisg to Loch Buie is an excursion well worth making (map on p. 23). In spring, the first wheatears are usually recorded here alongside calling curlew and displaying lapwing. At Loch Buie, the chaffinches will perch on your wing mirrors, hoping for a biscuit crumb. Fallow deer mingle with the red deer and cattle near the standing stones; snipe erupt from the marshy ground underfoot and woodcock and pheasants do the same in the woodland. You are never far from golden and white-tailed eagles at Loch Buie.

The tidal sea loch of Loch Don offers perhaps the most varied birding on the island. This is the area where I was first based when I started my first contract on Mull for the RSPB in 1984. I had just landed my ideal job and whilst the rare white-tailed eagles were our prime concern, we were based at Hazelbank Cottage in Lochdonhead on the edge of a beautiful and bird-filled sea loch. During the day we would scan the mudflats at low tide and then crane our necks skyward as a sub-adult sea eagle drifted over, causing panic amongst the waders and seaduck. It is at night that I like Loch Don best of all, standing outside on a star-filled night listening to the sounds of the feeding waders, the curlew calling and distant mallard and teal out on the mudflats. Happy memories!

The same scenario can still be played out today. Greenshank, redshank, teal, wigeon and shelduck feed eagerly as the tide moves in, common sandpipers call in summer from stones on the water's edge and ospreys are now regulars during the summer months. Take the road to Gorten from Lochdon and follow the road round the bay, stopping now and then to scan.

Curlew, Wigeon & Heron; Lochdon

① Where the mouth of the **Lussa River** opens into a broad, sheltered bay is the best place for wildfowl concentrations, especially outside the breeding season. These include moderate numbers of wintering Wigeon & Teal, & it is also a good time & place to see bobbing Dippers, down from their typical hill streams.

② This large roughly T-shaped sea loch has many attractions, not least a goodly population of Otters hunting its long, rocky shoreline for fish & crabs. There is also the year round presence of Eiders, &

a good chance of seeing eagles on the surrounding hilly skylines

③ **The western reaches** of the loch remain a great winter haunt of many seafowl, incl. Gt northern & Black-throated Divers, & Slavonian Grebe.

DUART POINT

CRAIGNURE

LOCH DON

GRASSPOINT

LOCH SPELVE

Shag - the 'shag' or crest, is only retained for a brief period in the spring.

kilometres, 1

1 miles

The single-track road has few places to stop and there is a small parking/turning area with good viewing just before the gate to Gorten farm. Or head over the beautiful little hump-backed bridge on the road to Grasspoint - a good road to walk or cycle along. This is good hen harrier country (winter and summer), sometimes short-eared and barn owls too. Red deer and feral goats graze out on the low ground, dipper may be seen near the bridge and in winter the occasional kingfisher finds this section of river to its liking. Red-breasted mergansers and little grebes are regulars here too. The Grasspoint road itself is narrow, steep and winding and not suitable for motorhomes, but there is a small car park down below Auchnacraig where you can wait a short while to watch for hunting harriers, sea eagles and buzzards. There is no parking further on towards Grasspoint itself, but a walk down here may reveal otters in the bay and sea eagles on the offshore skerries.

The road to Duart offers the chance of short-eared and barn

owls at dusk and the bay is worth a scan. At the castle itself, look out to sea for gannets towards Loch Linnhe and listen for occasional corncrakes in the iris and nettles.

East Mull is where journeys begin on Mull for most people visiting the island. The main terminal is at Craignure where the CalMac ferry from Oban docks. Even here, as the MV *Isle of Mull* steams in, you can sometimes watch otters feeding, dolphins accompanying the boat and eiders, black guillemot, shag and red-breasted mergansers on the water. It is not uncommon to see sea eagles overhead as the ferry comes in and if you head a little way to the north and park overlooking Scallastle Bay, you may see them sitting on the numerous offshore skerries. There are those who report watching sea eagles from the outdoor hot tub at the Isle of Mull Hotel! At the golf course in Scallastle Bay, the shingle beaches are home to a few waders and nesting terns in summer so please avoid walking along the coast here in June and July. They have a tough enough time of it avoiding the predations of mink.

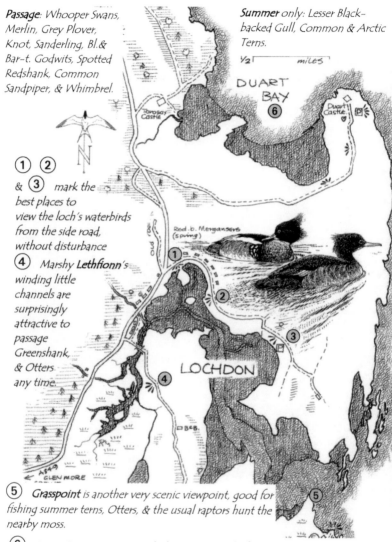

Birds **all year** round, include: Shag, Grey Heron, Mute Swan, Eider, Shelduck [except autumn], Mallard, Red-breasted Merganser, Hen Harrier, C. Buzzard, Redshank, O. Catcher, Ringed Plover, Snipe, Curlew, Common, Herring & Gt Blacked-back Gulls.

Passage: Whooper Swans, Merlin, Grey Plover, Knot, Sanderling, Bl.& Bar-t. Godwits, Spotted Redshank, Common Sandpiper, & Whimbrel.

Summer only: Lesser Black-backed Gull, Common & Arctic Terns.

½ ⌐ miles ⌐

DUART BAY
⑥

Torosay Castle

Duart Castle

① ② & ③ mark the best places to view the loch's waterbirds from the side road, without disturbance

④ Marshy **Lethfionn's** winding little channels are surprisingly attractive to passage Greenshank, & Otters any time.

Red-b. Mergansers (spring)

①

②

③

LOCHDON

④

B&B

← A849
GLEN MORE

⑤

⑤ **Grasspoint** is another very scenic viewpoint, good for fishing summer terns, Otters, & the usual raptors hunt the nearby moss.

⑥ Scenic **Duart Point** & Bay hold comparatively few birds, although it can be good for seawatching, & when many Red-b. Mergansers moult there,

Gazing up to the hills from the picnic area at Garmony, you may well see golden eagles over the ridge. Along the Garmony coast you will see greylag geese, newly established Canada geese, mute swan, curlew, heron and maybe porpoises off shore. In the conifer woodlands, jays and crossbills are occasionally heard but rarely seen.

To the north is Mull's second ferry port at Fishnish where ferries from Lochaline on the Morvern mainland arrive. This bay too is well worth a look. Herons nest in the adjoining forestry and fish along the shore. Shags, cormorants and gulls are always near the fish farm and the well-stocked bird feeders at the Secret Café near the slip attract siskins and a loyal flock of very tame chaffinches. Great-northern and red-throated divers may be offshore in the late winter and early spring. By May, the great-northern divers look stunning in their summer plumage but by the end of the month they have usually all headed north to their breeding grounds in Iceland.

Further north still and you reach Salen, Mull's epicentre, a perfect midway base for exploring the entire island. The old pier down Ardmore Road is a must, with the confiding shags, cormorants and gulls gracing the leaning pilings.

Salen Bay has three decaying boats, which must be the most photographed features on Mull. Otters are frequent in the bay and there is a parking area ¾ mile from the speed limit sign from which the bay can be scanned. Common seals haul out on the rocks in the bay and even have their pups there in summer - young animals swimming in the bay fool many of us looking hopefully for otters. Further along towards Tobermory another parking area, where there is a bench by a rowan tree, gives a view into Aros Bay. Wigeon, teal, mallard, heron, mergansers, dipper, greylag geese and goosanders are often seen in the estuary. The eastern seaboard of Mull offers many gentle but rewarding birding opportunities; you can stick with the waders and waterfowl of the coast or head inland and uphill into eagle and ptarmigan country.

East Mull Top Tips

An evening walk around Loch Don listening to the curlews.

Scan the Loch Don flood plain in winter for roosting hen harriers.

Search for summer-plumaged great-northern divers in May.

Stroll up Glen Forsa into the heart of eagle country.

Final Word

So there we have it. A whistle-stop tour of the wonderful islands of Mull and Iona. But they are places that deserve to be savoured and enjoyed in depth. Take your time if you possibly can. We hope this book has given you a small taste of what is on offer and we will certainly have missed some old favourites. That just means that there is even more for you to discover on your own. And a final plea: these islands and their wildlife are special because they are looked after by the people here and the wildlife is generally allowed to go about its business without disturbance. Let us all do our bit to help keep it that way.

Further Reading and Research

Jay Butler and Anna Levin, *The Wildlife of Mull and How to Find it*
Jay Butler and Anna Levin, *Was it a Whale?*
Mullarney et al, *Collins Bird Guide*
Alan Spellman, *The Isle of Mull Bird Report and Species List*
Philip Snow, *Light and Flight*
RSPB, *White-tailed Eagle, the Return of the Native*
www. rspb.org.uk/mull eagles
www.forestry.gov.uk/mullseaeagles
www.mullbirdclub.org.uk
www.mullbirds.com